GOD, PLEASE HELP ME FIND A JOB
21 Prayers for the Job Seeker

All scripture quotations are taken from

THE HOLY BIBLE

Scripture marked (NIV) NEW INTERNATIONAL VERSION
Scripture marked (KJV) KING JAMES VERSION
Scripture marked (NKJV) NEW KING JAMES VERSION
Scripture marked (GNT) GOOD NEWS TRANSLATION
Scripture marked (NLV) NEW LIVING TRANSLATION

Copyright 2020 by Sonia H Cameron

ISBN 978-1-7349724-0-5 paperback
ISBN 978-1-7349724-2-9 eBook
ISBN 978-1-7349724-1-2 Audio

PRAISE FOR "GOD, PLEASE HELP ME FIND A JOB: 21 PRAYERS FOR JOB SEEKERS

"*God, Please Help Me Find A Job* by Sonia H. Cameron has "Nailed It". This book is a great daily devotional for individuals who are looking to God during their employment search. This well-crafted writing will encourage seekers to remain focused on the main thing in life... your faith in the creator of all things. This dynamic manuscript offers concise guidance through finding gainful employment. While reading this anointed manual, not only was my faith in God stirred but I was further moved to seek my heavenly Father even the more.

I would absolutely, without hesitation, recommend this book to the unemployed and the employed alike."

— SHEPPARD FOUST, JR., PLANTER AND SENIOR PASTOR, NEW VISION CHRISTIAN CHURCH CENTER

"Readers will find 21 inspiration filled prayers that will invite them to keep the faith through the setbacks and disappointments that often accompany a job seeker's journey. Within each page the author not only offers spiritual support to uplift and encourage, but she also provides practical advice gleaned from her own personal and professional life as the Founder of Bless The Work, a website that uses Bible-based principles to encourage job seekers and employees. Now, after years of helping people through her website, Sonia H Cameron has written a book that will expand her message of hope for job seekers and serve as the first of many more books to come. "

— ANGELA JANUARY, CERTIFIED CAREER COACH

"As a Christian Woman and the CEO and founder of an Online Christian Ministry serving millions, I can say that this book by Sonia Cameron is well thought out and written, focusing on job seekers. She covered several situations but always seeking the guidance of God, foremost. It will touch and change lives for many."

— DR. JACQUELINE KING,
BLACK WOMEN EMPOWERED INCORPORATED

"Each prayer is compassionately and sensitively written. I especially feel it being attractive to unsaved and unchurched people, though it is beautifully Christian. It is not preachy but definitely very heart touching and magnetic."

— PASTOR SANDRA LILLY,
EAGLES'S SUMMIT CHRISTIAN FELLOWSHIP CHURCH

"*God, Please Help Me Find A Job!* offers hope to those currently unemployed or underemployed by demonstrating how prayer can serve as a prevailing source of encouragement, and also as the "secret" to an effective job search. Sonia makes it easy for readers to seek God and employment by giving them words to say when talking to God about their job search needs. While reading each prayer out loud, I was comforted by His presence. I recommend this book to anyone who is open to praying until their situation changes for the better."

— CAROLYN M. LYONS, MBA, PHR ~ LIFE COACH AND 25+ YEAR HUMAN RESOURCES PROFESSIONAL.

"I've only made it through the first few prayers, and I'm deeply moved by how relatable the prayers are. I think that this book will help many people be encouraged and hopeful, as well as understand the role our heavenly Father can play in our lives if we just ask."

— KEISHA WYNN, SUCCESS AND CAREER COACH

"Bravo to Author - Sonia H Cameron for answering the call to write *God, Please Help Me Find A Job* and moreover going to GOD for proven advice to support this need! She has covered each point in the job-seeking process supported by God's proven blueprint of prayer.

COVID-19 has driven Americans into a position of vulnerability. People and families who currently confront monetary hardship, need support through prayer as the journey of seeking employment continues. The assignment can be overwhelming when you understand that the joblessness numbers are expanding, and you are currently distinguished as a number rather than a certified competitor in the quest for work. Going to comfort through prayer and understanding that you will defeat this circumstance is the thing this book is about.

Personally, I lean toward 2 Corinthian 9:8 "8 "And God is able to bless you abundantly, so that in all things at all times, having all that you need, you will abound in every good work". We would all be able to breathe easy because of that sacred writing situated under prayer.

"*God, Please Help Me Find A Job* offers the job seeker inspiration through consistent prayers as we all go thru challenging times. With GOD, all things are possible if you trust and believe. "

— KIM BREWINGTON GORE,
NUCLEAR RECRUITING PROFESSIONAL

Dedication

I dedicate this book to the Trinity - The Father, The Son, and The Holy Spirit.

Table Of Contents

Introduction 11

SECTION 1: THE EMOTIONS OF THE JOBSEEKER
Fearful Job Seeker. 15
Anxious Job Seeker 17
Job Seeker With Low Self-esteem. 19
Depressed Job Seeker. 21

SECTION 2: THE STATUS OF THE JOB SEEKER
Brand New Job Seeker 25
Freelancer 27
The Fired Job Seeker 29
Long-time Job Seeker 31
Temporary Employee Who Wants Full-Time Employment. 33
Job Seeker with Financial Problems 35
When Jobs Are Scarce and Unemployment High 37

SECTION 3: THE NEEDS OF THE JOB SEEKER
Decision Making for Job Seekers 41
Job Seeker Wanting to Relocate 43
Changing Careers 45
Job Seeker Working Remotely 47
Needing a Breakthrough 49

SECTION 4: THE JOB SEARCH PROCESS
Job Seeker Who Needs Connections 53
Job Seeker's Resume .55
Preparing for the Interview 57

Job Offer	59
Giving Thanks for the Job	61
Job Seeker Who Desires to Walk in Excellence	63
It's Not Over!	65
Dedication	67
End Note	69
About the Author	71

Introduction

What gives me the authority to write this book?

My life experience...

In 2003 I found myself unemployed, recently diagnosed as being mentally ill, and separated from my husband. I did not want to file for disability because I'd rather live on "prosperity" Lane than on "I'm barely making it" Street. Besides all that, I had a 9-month-old baby to raise. I knew I needed to work and my only salvation in this situation was God.

During that season I learned about using scripture to pray and spending time in God's presence. I found another job in the corporate world, and I even revived my career. I understand what it's like to start over. I understand what it's like to spend days and weeks filling out applications. I can empathize with job seekers. I have felt anxiety and fear. I can relate to feelings of low-self esteem. The fear of not being smart enough or experienced enough, and especially the fear of being in the wrong demographic.

But, I discovered that having a relationship, and talking to God makes the search considerably less painful. In fact, your journey to find a job can be a blessing in disguise. Think of unemployment as an opportunity to reinvent yourself. Let the Creator be the designer that transitions you into an improved version of your best self.

Why did I write this book?

In America today, over 30 million people have filed for unemployment. Many need to find the means to make money for their bills. COVID-19 has created chaos in our economy!

I want to bring hope to the hopeless, help for the weary, and confidence to the person with low self-esteem. These prayers will lift job seekers to be all that God called them to be. These prayers will give the unemployed courage as they seek the face of God and employment. He lives inside each of us and longs to communicate with us.

The scripture-based prayers in this book give job seekers the words to say until they find their own voice. When we pray the word of God, we get results.

God says,

So shall my word be that goeth forth out of my mouth: it shall not return unto me void, but it shall accomplish that which I please, and it shall prosper in the thing whereto I sent it. Isaiah 55:11 (KJV)

I do not intend you to read this book in the order it's written. You can read any prayer in any order. In fact, I intend this book to be a pocket guide of prayers for job seekers. Keep it on your phone, ready to pull it up when needed.

Now, let's pray!

SECTION 1

The Emotions OF THE JOBSEEKER

When you find out you have lost your job, you start a grieving process. Only God can bring peace during that season. Jesus spoke to the storm and the winds and waves became still. The same is true of the storms of life; you must talk to God to understand and navigate the storm.

Fearful Job Seeker

Heavenly Father,

You are the most powerful God. You are my rock and my salvation. I have to be honest ; fear has taken over my thoughts lately. I know this fear is not an emotion that comes from You. And I know that faith in You is the remedy for fear. Thank you for changing the atmosphere of my life. Because of Your power inside of me, I am no longer afraid.

I will not fear famine.
I will not fear criticism.
I will overcome the thoughts of not being smart enough.
I am not afraid of economic reports, because You control my personal economy.
I am not scared of being in the wrong demographic.
I am determined to break past my fear of failure.
I am full of faith that I will get Your provision for a new position.
I know You will exceed my expectations. You keep all of Your promises!
I believe the scripture that says:

For I am the LORD your God who takes hold of your right hand and says to you. Do not fear; I will help you. Isaiah 41:13 (NIV)

In Jesus' Name, I pray.

Amen.

Anxious
JOB SEEKER

Heavenly Father,

You are the Alpha and Omega. I am anxious about my job search. I hate uncertain times like this.

Thank You for helping me relax and be at peace in this situation. I need You to deliver me from the fear You will expedite this job hunt.

Thank You for showing me how to overcome the worry of not having enough to survive during this time. I believe that You are showing me the way to change my uneasiness into a productive time in my life. You know how this transition will play out, and I trust You to lead me. My confidence rests in You. The more I talk to You, the stronger my faith gets.

Thank You for delivering me from the depths of fear and anxiety and lifting me higher so that I can praise You for the things to come. I believe *Psalm 34:4 (NIV)* that says, *I sought the Lord, and he answered me; he delivered me from all my fears.*

In Jesus' Name, I pray.

Amen.

JOB SEEKER WITH
Low Self-esteem

Lord,

You are a mighty God. There is no one else like You. I feel unqualified during this job search. I don't have enough skills. I don't have the right experiences. Certain reactions make me feel totally useless.

Only You can make me an employee in demand. Lord, show me how to make improvements and open the right doors of opportunity for me.

I yield to You, and I agree with Your word in 1 Peter 5:6-7 (NKJV): *Therefore humble yourselves under the mighty hand of God, that He may exalt you in due time, casting all your care upon Him, for He cares for you.*

In Jesus' Name, I pray.

Amen.

Depressed
JOB SEEKER

Lord God,

You are the only God of hope. I am in a dreary place mentally and emotionally. My thinking is off, and my confidence is low. I don't understand how I ended up in this place. I feel like I am being punished although I have done nothing wrong. I come to You because I feel I am at my wit's end. Help me to always remember that You love me and only have my best interest in mind.

Thank You for hearing my prayer and comforting me. I praise You even in this tough season.

As You give me the strength to go on, I will encourage others in need. I agree with *2 Corinthians 1:3-4 (NIV): Praise be to the God and Father of our Lord Jesus Christ, the Father of compassion and the God of all comfort, who comforts us in all our troubles, so that we can comfort those in any trouble with the comfort we ourselves receive from God.*

In Jesus' Name, I pray.

Amen.

SECTION 2

The Status OF THE JOB SEEKER

Your status determines your frame of mind. Believing that God will make your status temporary takes faith. Talking to God about your status gives you confidence that all will be well. Remember to trust God, and this too will pass.

Just like His promises are new every morning, I am expecting God to do a new thing in my career.

Brand New
JOB SEEKER

Father God,

Thank You for being the creator of all things good. I believe You created me for a positive purpose. The place where I thought I would receive payment for my time is no longer willing to employ me. I am clueless about what to do next, but I know that You will provide all that I need to get through this season.

Thank You for giving me ingenious ideas on how to provide a supply of money for my family. I am willing to do what it takes to succeed. Thank You for leading me to my next position.

I appreciate Your giving me a vision for my future and all that You have prepared for me. Hallelujah! I am thankful for Your support and Your blessings. With Your mighty power, You created the stars in the heavens, and I know You can create the perfect job for me.

As I seek employment, I remember Isaiah 40:26 (NIV):

Lift up your eyes and look to the heavens: Who created all these?

He who brings out the starry host one by one and calls forth each of them by name.

Because of his great power and mighty strength, not one of them is missing.

You are a powerful God who created all the stars and planets! I know You can lead me to a position designed with my skills, abilities, and talents in mind!

In Jesus' name, I pray.

Amen.

I am free like the sea and I lean on God to navigate my path.

Freelancer

Heavenly Father,

You are the original God. Thank You for giving me the skills and desire to be about "the grind".

I need Your blessings to succeed in every situation.

Give me a fresh approach as projects are presented. Thank You for allowing my contributions to be valued.

Let me be diplomatic when difficulties arise. Allow me to be a pleasure to work with, even on my worst days.

Give me the skill to swiftly negotiate the terms of employment.

Protect me as I work for each short term professional engagement. Don't let any harm come near me as I complete the gigs available to me.

Psalm 90:17 (GNT) says it best.

Lord our God, may your blessings be with us. Give us success in all we do!

All these blessings, I ask In Jesus' name.

Amen.

I cried to God and He heard my prayer.

The Fired
JOB SEEKER

Heavenly Father,

I praise You for being the God of redemption. You know they fired me! I am embarrassed and afraid of what will happen next.

Thank You for helping me analyze my work habits so that I understand where I failed. I will use this experience as a launching pad for greater success. Thank You for allowing me to transform my feelings of inadequacy into celebration for an assignment that uses my strengths. I need Your help in explaining my past. Let it be done with grace and professionalism. Thank You for Your infinite mercies.

I will work on my challenges so that my next employer will reap the benefits of this experience. I know You have a plan for me, and fresh opportunities are coming my way very soon. Like Job, I will praise You through the tough times. I agree with what Job said in Chapter 1, verse 21 (NIV): *Naked I came from my mother's womb, and naked I will depart.*

The Lord gave and the Lord has taken away; may the name of the Lord be praised.

I will rebound and rebuild my career. Lord, because of You, I have the victory in this situation!

In Jesus' Name, I pray.

Amen.

SONIA H CAMERON

Long-time JOB SEEKER

Heavenly Father,

Thank You for sending Your Son, Jesus Christ, to die for me. I am inspired by my hope in Him. I believe in his death and resurrection, and I trust in His power to bring dead things to life. I trust that Jesus will resurrect my career, and I know You specialize in giving life even when all seems lost.

I am thankful that out of the ashes of depression and fear will spring a new career containing hope, joy, and fulfillment. *Isaiah 61:3 (KJV)* says *To appoint unto them that mourn in Zion, to give unto them beauty for ashes, the oil of joy for mourning, the garment of praise for the spirit of heaviness; that they might be called trees of righteousness, the planting of the Lord, that he might be glorified.*

I thank You for making this come to pass in my life. Today I am Zion, I am Your child. I believe what it says in Your Word that I will have a praising heart instead of a debilitating spirit. I will be a person who will display Your magnificent beauty in word and deed. My life will be an example for everybody to see the exceptional things that happen when I trust God.

In Jesus' name. I pray.

Amen.

Temporary Employee
WHO WANTS FULL-TIME EMPLOYMENT

Father God,

You are the God Who supplies stability for the nations. I believe You will help me find full-time employment. I desire to have benefits and a salary.

Thank You for securing a position for me in a stable environment. I know there are a lot of uncertainties in the world today, but You are my rock.

I still expect a miracle. My faith is powerful, no matter the circumstance. I thank You for peace even when my status is unknown.

Thank You for Your promise in Hebrews 11:1 (NIV): *Now faith is confidence in what we hope for and assurance about what we do not see.*

In Jesus' Name, I pray.

Amen.

JOB SEEKER WITH *Financial Problems*

Dear God,

You are my great provider! My current financial situation is frustrating. I have a lengthy list of monetary needs, and the list gets longer every day. I need help from You, the powerful God of prosperity.

I repent for not taking advantage of every chance to give to others in the past, and I will do more to help others. Thank You for showing me how to activate the law of sowing and reaping: I must give to receive. Thank You for showing me what I have to give: time, money, advice, access to my contacts, clothes and anything else I have in my possession.

I must create opportunities for blessings to find me. I believe You are the God of the harvest. Thank You for multiplying the seeds I sow into other people. I now receive Your blessings!

Hallelujah!

I stand on Your word in *Luke 6:38 (NIV): Give, and it will be given to you. A good measure, pressed down, shaken together and running over, will be poured into your lap. For with the measure you use, it will be measured to you.*

In Jesus' Name, I pray.

Amen.

When Jobs Are Scarce
AND UNEMPLOYMENT HIGH

Father God,

You are the God of abundance, and I trust You. Looking at the job market, I know that jobs are scarce and unemployment is higher than it ever has been. You, however, are God of everything; so You are in control of the job market. I believe You can turn the tide just for me and allow me to walk in favor and blessing as I search for a job.

I understand that favor and access are more powerful than money. Thank You for giving me favor everywhere I apply and with the human resource associates. Thank You for the divine connections and contacts that can assist me in landing the right position.

Thank You for giving me strategies to get the access I need to communicate with hiring managers. I receive Your blessings. Even when everyone around me is experiencing defeat, I have all that I need to succeed. I trust in *2 Corinthians 9:8 (NIV)*: *And God is able to bless you abundantly, so that in all things at all times, having all that you need, you will abound in every good work.*

In Jesus' Name, I pray.

Amen

SECTION 3

The Needs OF THE JOB SEEKER

To find the right fit, you must know what you desire. Imagine yourself in the perfect situation. You must know what you need for your breakthrough! Most job seekers think it is all about compensation. However, there are other aspects of the job that bring satisfaction. Don't be afraid to talk to God about all of your needs during your job search.

Decision Making
FOR JOB SEEKERS

Heavenly Father,

You are the God of all seasons. Time moves at Your command. During this season in my life, I have many decisions to make. Help me to listen to the promptings of Your Holy Spirit. Thank You. He is inside me.

I need guidance in making budgeting decisions, financial decisions, health decisions, employment decisions, and family decisions. These areas in my life intertwine and affect one another.

Help me keep my eyes on You and focus on how my desires line up with Your will for my life. I praise You for enabling me to weigh the pros and cons of every step that I need to make.

Thank You for giving me discernment in every area of my life. I believe and trust in *Daniel 2:21 (NIV): He changes times and seasons; he deposes kings and raises up others. He gives wisdom to the wise and knowledge to the discerning.*

In Jesus' Name, I pray.

Amen.

*Just like for birds,
my career path is
navigated by God.*

JOB SEEKER
Wanting to Relocate

Father God,

You are the God of all wisdom. I need Your wisdom because I see myself prospering in a new location. Thank You for leading me to a fresh place where I have favor. As I follow Your lead, I will help and serve many people.

I receive the blessing You gave Abraham in *Genesis 12:1-3 (NIV)*:

Go from your country, your people and your father's household to the land I will show you.

I will make you into a great nation, and I will bless you;

I will make your name great, and you will be a blessing.

I will bless those who bless you, and whoever curses you I will curse;

and all peoples on earth will be blessed through you.

I will go where You want me to go!

In Jesus' Name, I pray.

Amen.

Like the tide, the God of the Universe determines my direction.

Changing CAREERS

Heavenly Father,

You are a faithful God. I praise You for the gifts and abilities You have given me. I feel that my strengths and weaknesses contradict the demands of my current job. I want to change careers, so I can reach my highest potential.

Thank You for Your support as I make this decision; I need Your guidance. You have known me since I was in my mother's womb, and You know what is best for me. I trust You to direct me to my next career where I will flourish.

I believe and agree with what David said in *Psalm 71:6-7 (NIV): From birth I have relied on You; You brought me forth from my mother's womb. I will ever praise You. I have become a sign to many; You are my strong refuge.*

Thank You for making me an example of what it means to become a sign to the world!

In Jesus' Name, I pray.

Amen.

I exceed expectations regardless of my location.

JOB SEEKER
Working Remotely

Lord God,

You are the God that makes good things come to pass. I believe that I am even more productive when I work remotely, and this is why I desire to work from home.

Lord, these are the reasons it is best for me to work remotely:

-I have a focused heart and an uncluttered mind.

-I work independently without supervision.

-Working remotely assists me with my work/life balance.

-For me, there are fewer distractions when I work from home.

I understand that working remotely is a sacred privilege. I vow not to abuse it, Lord.

I trust You to create an opportunity for me to work in a way that is beneficial to me and my employer. I believe Your promise in Psalm 37:4 (NKJV):

Delight yourself also in the Lord, And He shall give you the desires of your heart.

In Jesus' Name, I pray.

Amen.

NEEDING A *Breakthrough*

Father God,

Thank You for being the Master of the Breakthrough. I feel that the enemy blocks my efforts, and I am stuck. I believe only You can free me from this place. Thank You for providing me with hope for the future.

The enemy wants me to feel defeated, but he is under my feet! I know my breakthrough is coming soon!

I stand on Your promise in Lamentations 3:21-26 (NIV):

Yet this I call to mind and therefore I have hope:

Because of the Lord's great love, we are not consumed, for his compassions never fail.

They are new every morning; great is your faithfulness.

I say to myself, "The Lord is my portion; therefore I will wait for him."

The Lord is good to those whose hope is in him, to the one who seeks him; it is good to wait quietly for the salvation of the Lord.

In Jesus' Name, I pray.

Amen.

SECTION 4

THE JOB SEARCH
Process

One key to job search success is understanding the process. Most job seekers are not aware that one key to an effective search is relationships with people. The first step is to master networking, and then the rest of the search is down hill. However, the ultimate connection is God Almighty. Talking with Him makes seeking a job exponentially more effective than without prayer. God knows everyone. Knowing Him is a job search secret most people have not recognized as a factor in getting the job.

The remaining steps include:

Resume
Interview
Job Offer
Accepting the Position

Walking in Excellence

JOB SEEKER WHO
Needs Connections

Heavenly Father,

You are an all-knowing God. I need You to connect me with the people who will assist me with my job search. You know me and everything about them. You know the skills I need to connect with the right people.

Thank you for making me an excellent communicator so I can tell people how to help me. Lord, I believe I will recognize people who can solve a problem for me.

I pray that as I spend more time with You, You will connect me to those who have influence. You can give me favor with colleagues, human resource associates, and industry leaders. Thank You for the divine connections that will help me reach my destiny.

I believe John 15:7 (NIV): *If you remain in me and my words remain in you, ask whatever you wish, and it will be done for you.*

In Jesus' Name, I pray.

Amen.

I have a resume that floats to the top.

JOB SEEKER'S Resume

Heavenly Father,

You are the God of all authority! Thank You for giving me the right keywords so that my resume floats to the top. I believe that Your favor is on my name and my resume. I declare that, everywhere my name appears, there they favor it.

My resume will reflect my truth. I will not do any false advertising. I proclaim that Your grace is with every document I send out to prospective employers. I agree with Your thoughts in Proverbs 3:3 (NKJV):

Let not mercy and truth forsake you; Bind them around your neck,

Write them on the tablet of your heart,

And so find favor and high esteem In the sight of God and man.

In Jesus' Name, I pray.

Amen.

I have witty words and my ideas solve problems in the workplace.

PREPARING FOR THE

Father God,

You are the God of majesty! I need Your presence to go with me on this interview. Allow me to talk about my accomplishments and not just my experience.

Bless me to do effective research to prepare for the questions they will ask. I don't want to be the person who is just "winging it". Thank You for helping me communicate that I will deliver more than expected and on time.

I believe You will help me discern whether this organization is an excellent fit. Let me read clues from the environment and my potential colleagues. Allow them to recognize my value.

Proverbs 12:8 (NLV) precisely expresses my desire to be governed by Your wisdom: *A man will be praised for his wisdom, but a man with a sinful mind will be hated.*

In Jesus' Name, I pray.

Amen.

JOB Offer

Father God,

You are the God who lives within me, and I praise You. The most hard part of this search is waiting for something to happen. Sometimes it seems like time stands still and nothing moves forward.

Lord, I need Your grace to get me through this. Thank You for provoking me to make the best use of my time. Allow me to develop a strategy for negotiating the terms of employment. Thank You that my employer and I agree on a fair salary and benefits that match my experience.

There are many things I can accomplish while waiting for the job offer. There are still more people to connect and more skills to gain.

My faith is being perfected in this season. I am stronger than even I believe.

I trust in your word in Psalm 27:14 (NIV): *Wait for the Lord; be strong and take heart and wait for the Lord.*

In Jesus' Name, I pray.

Amen.

I give thanks and leap for joy because God has blessed me with a new job.

Giving Thanks
FOR THE JOB

Lord,

You are an awesome God!

Just saying "Thank You" is not enough to express my highest gratitude. I will forever praise Your name. I will always give You the glory for what you have done in my life and in my career.

I will be an example for You in the workplace because You blessed me. I am excited about the future because this journey has taught me to depend on You. With You, Lord, I always win!

Only You could have made this a peaceful transition into a booming career. God, You granted my request, and I am forever grateful. Your unmerited favor leaves me speechless.

I agree with Your word in 1 Chronicles 16:34 (NKJV): *Oh, give thanks to the Lord, for He is good! For His mercy endures forever.*

In Jesus' Name, I pray.

Amen.

JOB SEEKER WHO DESIRES TO Walk in Excellence

Dear God,

You are an excellent God! As Your child, I want to show that trait. I understand it takes work to go above and beyond the call of duty. I won't back down; I want to be an example of Your power and greatness.

Thank You for making me the best at what I do and giving me the ability to stand head and shoulders above my peers. I believe You will let others recognize that I am different because I walk in the spirit of excellence.

My goal is to be extraordinary in my field of work. I want to solve the principal problems that challenge everyone else. I will give all the glory and all the praise to You.

Daddy, I want to be just like You because *Psalm 150:2 (NKJV) says, Praise Him for His mighty acts; Praise Him according to His excellent greatness!*

In Jesus' Name, I pray.

Amen.

It's Not Over!

Thanks for praying these prayers. I know that you are on the road to getting your dream job. If you would like to continue on this encouragement path. You can receive support for your job hunt journey and engage with me on my website: https://blessthework.com

Receive a FREE download with practical job search tips you can implement to enhance your search.

About the Author

Sonia H. Cameron is a blogger who writes to encourage working people. She has written "Prayers for Your Career" as part of the https://blessthework.com website since 2010. On June 17, 2014, her first devotional article for Christian Devotions was published.

Sonia began her career in the corporate world as an intern with a local utility firm. She has had career ups and downs, and she loves to share them. Sonia is currently a technical support engineer with a corporation in Research Triangle Park, NC. She is married and has a blended family with wonderful children. Sonia loves to cook, and she also cooks to love.

You may contact Sonia via email at sonia@blessthework.com or via the website https://blessthework.com

www.ingramcontent.com/pod-product-compliance
Lightning Source LLC
Chambersburg PA
CBHW042130100526
44587CB00026B/4241

Dedication

Special Thanks To My Family, Friends, and Mentors who supported me through the journey of writing this manuscript:

Eula Turner, Bennie Cameron, Sr., Jordan Cameron, Tyson Cameron, Georgia Henry, Jonita Powell, Tomiko Ballard, Georjanne Rosa, Kayatta Shabbazz, Barbara Mitchell, Jovonte Henry, LaToya Cameron, LaTonya Cameron, BJ Cameron, Ida and Michael Pittman, Pamela Kelly, Corey McCall, Greg and Tina Henry, Kenya Allen, Joy Wilburn, Timothy Brewington, Kate and Zeb Baiye, Charrisse Nelson, Dr. Alfred Olabisi Tofade, Elizabeth Rogers, Ursula Howard, Deaundrea Adams, Pastor Nate and First Lady Tequilla Davis along with TNT Portraits.

End Note

If you have read this book and Jesus is not the Lord of your life, I invite you to make Him Lord and Saviour.

Pray this prayer:

Lord Jesus,

I repent of my sins, please come into my heart. I want You to be my Lord and Savior. I believe Romans 10:9 (NKJV): *If you confess with your mouth the Lord Jesus and believe in your heart that God has raised Him from the dead, you will be saved.*

Thank You for making me Your child and allowing me to join the body of believers.

Congratulations and welcome to the family of believers!